JACQUELINE KENNEDY ONASSIS

A LIFE OF ELEGANCE AND INFLUENCE

WRITTEN BY:

OLIVIER SCOFFIELD

TABLE OF CONTENTS

INTRODUCTION

Jacqueline Lee Kennedy Onassis, born Jacqueline Bouvier, was a remarkable American figure known for her multifaceted talents and her role as the beloved first lady of the United States from 1961 to 1963, as the wife of President John F. Kennedy. She captured the hearts of the American public with her unwavering dedication to her family and her passionate commitment to preserving the historical significance of the White House and other landmarks. Jacqueline's deep interest in American history, culture, and the arts further endeared her to the nation, and she became a renowned international fashion icon and a respected cultural ambassador for the United States.

After earning a Bachelor of Arts in French literature from George Washington University in 1951, Bouvier kick started her career as an inquiring photographer at the Washington Times-Herald. It was at a dinner party in Washington where she first encountered Congressman John F. Kennedy, who later became a Senator. The two tied the knot on September 12, 1953, in Newport, Rhode Island, and they were blessed with four children, though two sadly passed away in infancy. When her husband assumed the presidency in 1960, Jacqueline made headlines for her prominent efforts to restore and revitalize the White House, emphasizing its significance in arts and culture while also showcasing her impeccable sense of style. Remarkably, at the age of 31, she became the third-youngest first lady of the United States and was recognized as Time magazine's Woman of the Year in 1962.

Beyond her domestic role, Jacqueline's work as a cultural ambassador played a pivotal role in enhancing U.S. foreign relations and diplomacy.

Through her extensive travels, she sought to foster cross-cultural understanding and respect, using her linguistic skills in French, Spanish, and Italian to connect with foreign audiences on a more personal level. Her impactful speeches resonated well, earning praise for their eloquence, and played a significant role in strengthening relationships between the United States and other nations. One particularly successful venture was her "goodwill" tour of India and Pakistan in 1962, accompanied by her sister, Princess Lee Radziwill, which left a lasting positive impression on foreign leaders, including the notoriously difficult figures, Charles de Gaulle and Nikita Khrushchev.

As the first lady, Jacqueline spearheaded a major restoration project of the White House state rooms, replacing modern furnishings with authentic period pieces and art from the White House collection. Collaborating with a team of experts, she aimed to showcase the presidency in a culturally significant setting akin to official residences in Europe. Her dedication to this endeavor turned the White House into a vital museum of American history, with a special emphasis on the performing arts, solidifying its status as an essential cultural institution.

Jacqueline Lee Kennedy Onassis left an enduring legacy, not only as an influential first lady but also as a woman of intellect, artistic appreciation, and cross-cultural bridging, forever etching her name in history and the hearts of people worldwide.

In 1961, President Kennedy supported a law that declared White House collection items of historical or artistic value as official White House property. To preserve presidential history, Jacqueline Kennedy founded the White House Historical Association (WHHA) and funded it in part through the sale of the first White House guidebook, "The

White House: An Historic Guide." This guidebook has been continuously updated, along with other WHHA publications, exhibits, and educational programs, all celebrating the profound cultural significance of the White House.

After an Emmy-winning televised tour of her White House restoration work in 1962, Jacqueline focused on preserving Lafayette Square, near the White House. She advocated for preserving existing structures and reconsidering new construction plans to honor the Square's heritage, leading to its inclusion in the National Register of Historic Places in 1970.

Jacqueline's impact extended to the arts and culture, influencing her husband's creation of committees and organizations, such as the President's Advisory Committee on the Arts, the National Council on the Arts, and the National

Endowment for the Arts and Humanities. She and President Kennedy also supported the establishment of the John F. Kennedy Memorial Center for the Performing Arts in 1971.

After President Kennedy's assassination, Jacqueline became a UNESCO Goodwill Ambassador from 1965 to 1977, advocating for cultural preservation to promote cross-cultural understanding. Her efforts garnered international support for preserving historic sites like the Angkor temples in Cambodia and the relocation of the Temple of Dendur to the Metropolitan Museum of Art in 1978.

Jacqueline Kennedy's dedication to history, culture, and the arts left a lasting impact on the White House, Lafayette Square, and the preservation of cultural treasures both nationally and internationally.

After the assassination of Robert Kennedy in 1968, Jacqueline Kennedy sought solace from the troubled state of America by marrying Greek shipping magnate Aristotle Onassis. This decision drew mixed reactions, with some preferring to remember her solely as President Kennedy's widow, rather than the glamorous "Jackie O" portrayed in the media. After Onassis passed away in 1975, Jacqueline returned to work as a book editor and continued her dedication to historic preservation. Notably, she played a crucial role in saving Grand Central Station from demolition in 1975.

In 1979, the John F. Kennedy Presidential Library and Museum was established in Boston, an event Jacqueline attended. She later embarked on a romantic relationship with Maurice Tempelsman, a longtime acquaintance and diamond merchant. Despite facing health challenges in the early 1990s, Jacqueline remained active in various pursuits.

Sadly, she was diagnosed with non-Hodgkin lymphoma in 1994. Despite an initially hopeful prognosis, the cancer progressed rapidly, and she chose to forgo further treatment. Surrounded by her loved ones, Jacqueline passed away on May 19, 1994. After a private family funeral in New York, she was laid to rest alongside President Kennedy and their two infant children in Arlington National Cemetery. President Clinton delivered a moving eulogy, highlighting her role as a devoted mother.

Even after her death, Jacqueline Onassis remains an enduring figure in American history. Her personal effects were auctioned in 1996, adding millions to her estate. She was admired by many, listed among Gallup's Most-Admired Men and Women of the 20th century in 1999. The Metropolitan Museum of Art paid tribute to her iconic style in 2001 with a special exhibition during the Met Gala. Her legacy also continues in popular culture, as seen in the film "Jackie," which earned an Academy Award nomination for Natalie Portman's portrayal of Jacqueline Onassis. Moreover, historians consistently hold her in high regard, according to surveys conducted since 1982. Jacqueline's impact as a first lady and cultural figure endures, leaving a lasting impression on the nation's memory.

1929–61: EARLY YEARS
FAMILY AND CHILDHOOD

Jacqueline Lee Bouvier was born on July 28, 1929, in Southampton, New York, to John Vernou "Black Jack" Bouvier III, a Wall Street stockbroker, and Janet Norton Lee, a socialite of Irish descent. Raised in the Roman Catholic faith, she spent her early years in Manhattan and at the family's country estate in East Hampton, known as Lasata.

Jacqueline admired her father, who favored her over her younger sister, Caroline Lee. His praise and positive attitude towards her contributed to Jacqueline's early confidence and independence. She was an enthusiastic equestrian and excelled in horse-riding competitions, a passion she carried throughout her life. Besides horse-riding, Jacqueline enjoyed ballet, reading, and learning foreign languages, with a particular focus on French.

She attended Manhattan's Chapin School from grades 1 to 7, where she proved to be a bright student. However, she occasionally misbehaved, mainly out of boredom after finishing assignments ahead of her classmates. Her behavior improved after receiving advice from the headmistress on the importance of good conduct.

The Bouvier family faced challenges in their marriage due to her father's alcoholism, extramarital affairs, and financial difficulties following the Wall Street Crash of 1929. They separated in 1936 and divorced four years later, drawing public attention to their personal lives. The divorce had a profound impact on Jacqueline, leading her to retreat into a private world of her own.

Her mother, Janet, later married Hugh Dudley Auchincloss Jr., an heir to Standard Oil. Unfortunately, Jacqueline and her sister couldn't attend the wedding due to travel restrictions during World War II. From this marriage, Jacqueline gained three step-siblings: Hugh "Yusha" Auchincloss III, Thomas Gore Auchincloss, and Nina Gore Auchincloss. She developed a close bond with Yusha, who became one of her most trusted confidants. The marriage also brought two more half-siblings, Janet Jennings Auchincloss in 1945 and James Lee Auchincloss in 1947.

After Jacqueline's mother remarried, the Merrywood estate in McLean, Virginia, belonging to her stepfather, became their main residence. However, they also spent time at his other estate, Hammersmith Farm in Newport, Rhode Island, as well as her father's homes in New York City and

Long Island. Despite this transition, Jacqueline developed a close relationship with her stepfather, considering him a paternal figure who provided her with stability and a privileged childhood.

She attended Chapin School for seven years before moving on to Holton-Arms School in Washington, D.C., from 1942 to 1944, and then Miss Porter's School in Connecticut from 1944 to 1947. Choosing Miss Porter's allowed her to distance herself from the Auchincloss family and emphasized college preparatory classes. Jacqueline was known for her wit, horsemanship, and her determination not to become a mere housewife.

COLLEGE AND CAREER START-UP

In 1947, she began her college education at Vassar College in Poughkeepsie, New York, a women's institution at the time. While academically accomplished, she disliked the isolated location and often traveled back to Manhattan for weekends and social events. During her junior year, she studied abroad in France at the University of Grenoble and the Sorbonne, part of a program through Smith College.

After returning to the United States, Jacqueline transferred to George Washington University in Washington, D.C., where she graduated with a Bachelor of Arts degree in French literature in 1951. During her early marriage to John F. Kennedy, she also took continuing education classes in American history at Georgetown University.

At George Washington University, Jacqueline won a junior editorship at Vogue magazine, but her time there was short-lived. Advised to quit by the managing editor due to concerns about her marriage prospects at 22 years old, she left after just one day of work. Jacqueline's eventful life and experiences were captured in her only autobiography, "One Special Summer," co-authored with her sister Lee, which also showcased her drawings.

Despite the brief stint at Vogue, Jacqueline's legacy as a well-educated, accomplished, and stylish woman would endure and play a significant role in her later public life as the First Lady of the United States.

After returning to Merrywood, Jacqueline Bouvier found work as a part-time receptionist at the Washington Times-Herald, thanks to a family friend's recommendation. However, her ambition led her to request more challenging work, and she was assigned to the city editor as an "Inquiring Camera Girl." Despite her lack of experience, she impressed her colleagues with her wit and attractiveness. Her job involved approaching random people on the street, posing clever questions, and capturing their pictures for publication alongside their responses.

During this time, Jacqueline briefly became engaged to a stockbroker named John Husted. However, the engagement was short-lived, lasting only a month, as she found him immature and uninteresting after getting to know him better.

BETROTHMENT TO JOHN KENNEDY

In May 1952, Jacqueline was formally introduced to U.S. Representative John F. Kennedy through a mutual friend. She was immediately drawn to his charm, wit, wealth, and shared interests, such as their Catholic background, love for reading, and previous experiences living abroad. Despite Kennedy's busy schedule running for the U.S. Senate seat, their relationship grew more serious, and he proposed to her after the November election.

The couple's wedding took place on September 12, 1953, at St. Mary's Church in Newport, Rhode Island, and it was a grand social event attended by numerous guests. They honeymooned in Acapulco, Mexico, and settled in their new home, Hickory Hill, in McLean, Virginia.

In the early years of their marriage, both Jacqueline and John faced personal challenges. John battled with Addison's disease and chronic back pain, while Jacqueline suffered a miscarriage and gave birth to a stillborn daughter named Arabella in 1956. Despite these setbacks, the couple maintained a strong bond and warm relationship with John's parents, Joseph and Rose Kennedy.

Later, they sold Hickory Hill to John's brother, Robert, and moved to Georgetown, where they resided in a townhouse. Additionally, they had a permanent residence in Boston at 122 Bowdoin Street during John's congressional career. Despite the difficulties, their love and partnership endured, shaping the course of history as John F. Kennedy became the President of the United States and Jacqueline Kennedy assumed the role of the nation's First Lady.

On November 27, 1957, Jacqueline gave birth to their daughter, Caroline. During this time, John was running for re-election to the Senate, and they appeared on the cover of Life magazine with their newborn daughter. Together, they campaigned during the re-election efforts, with Jacqueline's presence drawing larger crowds and adding value to John's campaign. She was credited with playing a vital role in securing his victory in the 1958 election.

Despite her shyness and discomfort with too much attention, Jacqueline's visibility in ads and campaign events proved crucial for John's success. Her support and advice extended beyond the campaign, as she also helped improve his wardrobe in preparation for his upcoming presidential bid.

In 1959, historian Arthur M. Schlesinger visited the Kennedy Compound in Hyannis Port and had a conversation with Jacqueline. He was struck by her tremendous awareness, keen judgment, and insightful observations. During John's travels to 14 states that year, Jacqueline took breaks to spend time with their daughter and also provided valuable counsel to her husband. For instance, she traveled to Louisiana to garner support for his presidential campaign.

As the couple prepared for the presidential campaign, Jacqueline's involvement and support became increasingly significant, foreshadowing her essential role as First Lady during John F. Kennedy's presidency.

1961–63: FIRST LADY OF THE UNITED STATES
ADVOCATING FOR PRESIDENCY

On January 3, 1960, John F. Kennedy officially announced his candidacy for the presidency, starting his nationwide campaign. Jacqueline Kennedy accompanied him to campaign events in the early months of the election year, attending whistle-stops and dinners together. However, when she became pregnant, she decided to stay at home in Georgetown due to her previous high-risk pregnancies.

Despite not physically participating in the campaign, Jacqueline remained actively involved by writing a weekly syndicated newspaper column, Campaign Wife, responding to correspondence, and giving media interviews. Her fashion choices also drew significant attention, with both admiration for her personal style and criticism for her preference for French designers and spending on her wardrobe. To downplay her wealthy background, she emphasized her campaign work and refrained from discussing her clothing choices publicly.

On July 13, 1960, at the Democratic National Convention in Los Angeles, John F. Kennedy was nominated as the party's presidential candidate. Due to her pregnancy, Jacqueline did not attend the nomination, which had been publicly announced ten days earlier. Instead, she watched the first televised presidential debate between her husband and Republican candidate Richard Nixon from their home in Hyannis Port.

In preparation for the third debate on October 13, Jacqueline sought the aid of Arthur Schlesinger and

John Kenneth Galbraith to provide her husband with new ideas and speeches. She also appeared alongside John for a joint interview on Person to Person on September 29, 1960. Throughout the campaign, Jacqueline's grace, style, and intelligence captivated the public, and she became an integral part of the Kennedy campaign's public image.

THE FIRST LADY OF THE UNITED STATES

After John F. Kennedy's narrow victory over Richard Nixon in the presidential election on November 8, 1960, Jacqueline Kennedy gave birth to their first son, John F. Kennedy Jr., on November 25. Her hospital stay and the details of both her and the baby's condition became a subject of intense media interest, marking the first instance of national fascination with the Kennedy family.

On January 20, 1961, John F. Kennedy was sworn in as the president of the United States, and at 31 years old, Jacqueline became the third youngest first lady in history. As a presidential couple, the Kennedys were unique for their youth, political affiliation, and media presence. They were seen as a perfect fit for the cool, TV-oriented culture of the early 1960s.

Jacqueline's fashion choices continued to be a topic of discussion, and she became a trendsetter, hiring American designer Oleg Cassini to create her wardrobe. She was the first first lady to have a press secretary and managed her interactions with the media carefully, protecting her privacy and that of her children.

Despite stating that her priority was taking care of her husband and children, Jacqueline also dedicated herself to promoting American arts and preserving its history. The restoration of the White House was her main project, and she also hosted social events that brought together influential figures from politics and the arts. She wanted to establish a Department of the Arts, but her efforts contributed to the establishment of the National Endowment for the Arts and the National Endowment for the Humanities during Lyndon B. Johnson's presidency. Jacqueline's charm, elegance, and cultural interests won her widespread positive public attention and garnered international support for the Kennedy administration's policies during the Cold War.

RESTORATION OF THE WHITE HOUSE

Before becoming the first lady, Jacqueline Kennedy had visited the White House twice: once as a grade-school tourist in 1941 and again as a guest of outgoing First Lady Mamie Eisenhower shortly before her husband's inauguration. On her second visit, she was disappointed to find that the mansion's rooms were furnished with undistinguished pieces that lacked historical significance. This prompted her first major project as first lady – restoring the White House's historical character.

Upon moving into the White House, she began her restoration efforts with the help of interior decorator Sister Parish. She made the family quarters more suitable for family life by adding a kitchen and new rooms for her children. To fund the restoration, she established a fine arts committee and published a White House guidebook, with sales proceeds used for the project.

Beyond the White House, Jacqueline Kennedy also oversaw the redesign and replanting of the Rose Garden and the East Garden, which was later renamed the Jacqueline Kennedy Garden. She was also instrumental in saving historic homes in Lafayette Square in Washington, D.C., recognizing their significance in the nation's capital.

Her dedication to historic preservation extended internationally as well. She brought attention to the threatened 13th-century B.C. temples of Abu Simbel in Egypt, which were in danger of being flooded by the Aswan Dam.

To enrich the White House with historical furnishings, she personally contacted possible donors and initiated a bill establishing that White House furnishings would become property of the Smithsonian Institution. This prevented departing presidents from taking items with them, preserving historical pieces for future generations.

Her commitment to preserving White House history led to the establishment of several organizations, including the White House Historical Association, the Committee for the Preservation of the White House, and the position of a permanent White House curator. She became the first presidential spouse to hire a curator for the White House. Jacqueline Kennedy's passion for historical preservation left a lasting legacy, ensuring that the White House and its treasures would be preserved and celebrated for generations to come.

On February 14, 1962, Jacqueline Kennedy, accompanied by Charles Collingwood of CBS News, took American television viewers on a captivating tour of the White House. During the tour, she expressed her strong belief that the White House should showcase a fine collection of American art, emphasizing its significance as the backdrop for the presidency and its representation to the world. She wanted the American people to take pride in their rich cultural heritage and believed the White House should be the ideal place to showcase it to foreign visitors.

The televised tour garnered immense popularity, with an impressive 56 million viewers in the United States tuning in to watch. The film was also distributed to 106 countries, reaching audiences worldwide. Her efforts in presenting the White House's cultural importance and beauty earned her a special Academy of Television Arts & Sciences

Trustees Award at the 1962 Emmy Awards. This recognition made her the first and only first lady to win an Emmy award for her outstanding contribution to television.

Jacqueline Kennedy's tour of the White House not only displayed her love for American art and history but also highlighted her ability to captivate and engage the public through the new medium of television. Her dedication to preserving and promoting American culture and arts left a lasting impact, inspiring millions of viewers both at home and abroad.

INTERNATIONAL TRAVELS

Jacqueline Kennedy, the First Lady of the United States, was not only known for her grace and elegance but also for her cultural and diplomatic contributions on the global stage. She served as a cultural ambassador, traveling to various countries to promote cultural exchange and strengthen diplomatic relations. With her fluency in multiple languages, including French, Spanish, and Italian, and her extensive cultural knowledge, she established strong relationships with foreign leaders and delivered speeches in different countries.

Her impact was particularly significant in France, where she visited with President Kennedy in 1961. During the trip, she impressed the French people with her ability to speak in their native language and her deep understanding of French history and culture. Her visit was deemed a great success, and she received widespread praise for her eloquence and charm.

Throughout her husband's presidency, Jacqueline Kennedy undertook many official visits to other countries, both on her own and alongside the President. Despite initial concerns about her political appeal, she won the hearts of international dignitaries with her intelligence and cultural fluency.

In addition to France, she toured other countries such as Austria, India, and Pakistan, leaving a lasting impression wherever she went. The President of Pakistan gifted her a horse named Sardar, a testament to the strong rapport she developed with foreign leaders.

Jacqueline Kennedy's contributions as a cultural ambassador were highly valued, and she played a crucial role in enhancing cultural diplomacy and strengthening ties between the United States and other nations. Her language skills, knowledge, and charisma made her an influential figure in international relations, and she remains a revered and admired figure in the history of first ladies.

DEATH OF A CHILD

In early 1963, Jacqueline Kennedy found herself expecting another child, and in response, she scaled back her official duties. During the summer, she sought refuge at a rented home on Squaw Island near the Kennedy compound on Cape Cod, Massachusetts. However, on August 7, several weeks before her due date, she went into labor and gave birth to a son, Patrick Bouvier Kennedy, through an emergency Caesarean section at Otis Air Force Base nearby. Unfortunately, Patrick's lungs were not fully developed, and he was transferred to Boston Children's Hospital, where he tragically passed away just two days after birth due to hyaline membrane disease.

Jacqueline Kennedy remained at the Air Force Base to recover from the Caesarean delivery, while her husband, President Kennedy, went to Boston to be with their son during his final moments. On August 14, the President returned to the base to bring her home and express his gratitude to the nurses and airmen who had taken care of her during her stay. In appreciation, she gifted them framed and signed lithographs of the White House.

The loss of their son had a profound impact on the First Lady, leading her to experience a period of depression. However, the tragedy also strengthened the bond between Jacqueline and John Kennedy, bringing them closer together in their shared grief. Although initially hesitant, the President allowed Jacqueline to visit her friend Aristotle Onassis on his yacht to aid in her recuperation. The trip received considerable disapproval from the public, the Kennedy administration, and Congress. Nevertheless, Jacqueline returned to the United States on October 17, 1963, acknowledging that she regretted being away for as long as she had but had needed time to cope with her melancholy following the loss of their baby.

ASSASSINATION OF JOHN F. KENNEDY

On November 21, 1963, President John F. Kennedy and First Lady Jacqueline Kennedy embarked on a political trip to Texas. This was the first time she had joined her husband on such an excursion within the United States. The next day, November 22, they took a short flight from Fort Worth to Dallas, where they were to attend a lunch at the Trade Mart. Jacqueline was wearing a bright pink Chanel suit and a pillbox hat, a personal choice of the President's.

As their motorcade turned on Elm Street in Dealey Plaza, the First Lady heard what she initially thought were motorcycle backfires. It was only after hearing Governor Connally's scream that she realized they were gunshots. Within seconds, her husband was struck in the head. Jacqueline, reacting quickly, attempted to climb onto the back of the limousine. Secret Service agent Clint Hill rushed to her aid and directed her back to her seat. A photograph taken by Ike Altgens captured this moment and made headlines worldwide.

The President was rushed to Parkland Hospital, and Jacqueline requested to be present in the operating room. However, despite the medical team's efforts, President Kennedy did not regain consciousness and passed away at the age of 46. After his death was confirmed, Jacqueline refused to change out of her blood-stained clothing. She wanted the world to see the terrible impact of her husband's assassination and reportedly regretted washing the blood off her face and hands. She boarded Air Force One alongside Vice President Lyndon B. Johnson, still wearing the blood-stained pink suit. This suit later became a symbol of the tragedy and was eventually donated to the National Archives and Records Administration.

During Johnson's swearing-in as president, Jacqueline was present at his side. Her presence was seen as a way to demonstrate the legitimacy of the transition of power to JFK's loyalists and the world. The assassination deeply affected Jacqueline Kennedy, and her strength and resilience during that tragic time left a lasting impact on the nation's memory.

After the assassination of President John F. Kennedy, Jacqueline Kennedy took an active role in planning his state funeral, drawing inspiration from Abraham Lincoln's funeral service. She insisted on a closed casket, overriding the wishes of her brother-in-law, Robert Kennedy. The funeral was held at the Cathedral of St. Matthew the Apostle in Washington D.C., and the burial took place at Arlington National Cemetery.

During the funeral procession, Jacqueline led on foot and personally lit the eternal flame at the gravesite, a feature she requested to honor her husband's memory. Her composure and grace during the funeral earned her praise and admiration, with Lady Jeanne Campbell remarking that Jacqueline had brought majesty to the American people during their time of grief.

A week after the assassination, President Lyndon B. Johnson established the Warren Commission, headed by Chief Justice Earl Warren, to investigate the assassination. The Commission's report, issued ten months later, concluded that Lee Harvey Oswald had acted alone. Privately, Jacqueline expressed little interest in the investigation, believing that even if they had the right suspect, it would not bring her husband back. Despite her reservations, she cooperated and provided a deposition to the Warren Commission.

Following the funeral and the intense media coverage surrounding her, Jacqueline retreated from the public eye, except for a brief appearance to honor Secret Service agent Clint Hill, who had tried to shield her and the President during the assassination. Her focus shifted towards protecting her children and maintaining privacy during their time of mourning.

1963–75: LIFE FOLLOWING THE ASSASSINATION
MOURNING AND LATER PUBLIC APPEARANCES

Don't let it be forgot, that once there was a spot, for one brief, shining moment that was known as Camelot.

There'll be great presidents again ... but there will never be another Camelot.

After the assassination of President John F. Kennedy, Jacqueline Kennedy gave an interview to Theodore H. White of Life magazine in which she compared her husband's presidency to King Arthur's mythical Camelot. She mentioned that President Kennedy often played the title song from the musical "Camelot" before going to bed, and she quoted lines from the musical to express her feelings of loss. This comparison led to the era of the Kennedy administration being referred to as the "Camelot Era," although some historians later argued that the comparison was not entirely appropriate.

In the aftermath of her husband's death, Jacqueline and her children remained in the White House for two weeks before leaving. President Lyndon B. Johnson offered her an ambassadorship to France as a gesture of kindness, but she declined the offer along with subsequent offers for ambassadorships to Mexico and the United Kingdom. She spent most of 1964 in mourning, making few public appearances.

Kennedy oversaw the establishment of the John F. Kennedy Presidential Library and Museum, which serves as the repository for official papers from the Kennedy administration. She also attended selected memorial dedications to her late husband and was involved in legal battles to protect her husband's public image, notably in the case of William Manchester's book, "The Death of a President."

During the Vietnam War, Kennedy traveled to Cambodia with David Ormsby-Gore, a former British ambassador to the United States during the Kennedy administration. Her visit to Cambodia was seen as a significant step in repairing Cambodian-US relations. She also attended the funeral services of Martin Luther King Jr. in Atlanta, Georgia, in April 1968, despite her initial reluctance due to the emotional reminders of her husband's death.

RELATIONSHIP WITH ROBERT F. KENNEDY

After the assassination of President John F. Kennedy, Jacqueline Kennedy relied heavily on her brother-in-law Robert F. Kennedy for support. She saw him as the least like his father of the Kennedy brothers and considered him a source of comfort and strength, especially during difficult times such as her miscarriage early in her marriage. After her husband's death, Robert became a surrogate father to her children, providing them with guidance and support.

When the Tet offensive in Vietnam led to a drop in President Lyndon B. Johnson's poll numbers, Robert Kennedy's advisors encouraged him to enter the presidential race. Jacqueline met with him during this time and encouraged him to run for president, despite her concerns about his safety and the strong public dislike he faced. She campaigned for him and supported his candidacy, even expressing optimism that Kennedy would once again occupy the White House through his victory.

However, tragedy struck again on June 5, 1968, when Robert Kennedy was mortally wounded by an assassin just moments after celebrating his victory in the California Democratic presidential primary. Jacqueline Kennedy rushed to his side at the hospital, joining other Kennedy family members, but he never regained consciousness and passed away the following day at the age of 42. His death was a devastating loss for Jacqueline and the entire Kennedy family.

MARRIAGE TO ARISTOTLE ONASSIS

After the assassination of Robert F. Kennedy in 1968, Jacqueline Kennedy reportedly experienced a relapse of the depression she had suffered after her husband's death nearly five years earlier. She became fearful for her own life and the safety of her two children, feeling that they might also be targeted. This fear led her to consider leaving the United States for increased privacy and security.

On October 20, 1968, Jacqueline Kennedy married Aristotle Onassis, a Greek shipping magnate and her longtime friend. The wedding took place on his private Greek island, Skorpios. After the marriage, she legally changed her name to Jacqueline Onassis and lost her right to Secret Service protection as the widow of a U.S. president. The marriage drew significant adverse publicity, with criticism from some quarters, and she was followed by paparazzi and given the nickname "Jackie O."

During her marriage to Onassis, Jacqueline Onassis was appointed as the vice president of the Newport Restoration Foundation, a role she championed publicly. She and Onassis lived in several different residences, including her Fifth Avenue apartment in Manhattan, his properties in Paris and Greece, his private island Skorpios, and his yacht Christina O. She maintained a close relationship with Ted Kennedy, and he often visited her and her children during this time.

After Onassis's health declined rapidly and he passed away in 1975, Jacqueline Onassis faced legal challenges over his estate. In the end, she accepted a settlement of $26 million from his daughter Christina Onassis and waived all other claims to the Onassis estate.

1975–90s: LATER YEARS

After the death of Aristotle Onassis, Jacqueline Onassis returned permanently to the United States and split her time between Manhattan, Martha's Vineyard, and the Kennedy compound in Hyannis Port, Massachusetts. In 1975, she took on a new role as a consulting editor at Viking Press, where she worked for two years.

For almost a decade, Onassis avoided participating in political events, but she surprised many when she attended the 1976 Democratic National Convention and appeared in the visitors' gallery. She resigned from Viking Press in 1977 after facing criticism for the publication of a novel that depicted a fictional assassination plot against Ted Kennedy. In the years that followed, she showed support for Ted Kennedy's presidential campaign, attending events alongside her mother-in-law, Rose Kennedy.

After resigning from Viking Press, Onassis joined Doubleday as an associate editor, working under John Turner Sargent, Sr. She edited various books for the company, including Larry Gonick's The Cartoon History of the Universe, Naghib Mahfuz's Cairo Trilogy, Gelsey Kirkland's autobiography, Carly Simon's autobiography, and Diana Vreeland's autobiography. She also encouraged Dorothy West, a neighbor on Martha's Vineyard, to complete her novel The Wedding, a significant work about race, class, wealth, and power in the United States.

In addition to her work as an editor, Jacqueline Onassis was actively involved in cultural and architectural preservation efforts. In the 1970s, she played a key role in the campaign to save Grand Central Terminal from demolition and worked on its renovation in Manhattan. A plaque inside the terminal recognizes her significant contribution to its preservation. She also participated in protests against a planned skyscraper at Columbus Circle in the 1980s, which would have cast shadows on Central Park. As a result of the protests, the project was canceled. She was also involved in the preservation of Olana, the home of Frederic Edwin Church in upstate New York.

Throughout this time, Onassis continued to receive considerable press attention, especially from the paparazzi photographer Ron Galella. He followed her and took candid photos without her permission, leading her to obtain a restraining order against him and drawing attention to the issue of paparazzi intrusion.

From 1980 until her death, Onassis had a close relationship with Maurice Tempelsman, a

Belgian-born industrialist and diamond merchant who also served as her companion and financial adviser.

In the early 1990s, Onassis supported Bill Clinton and contributed to his presidential campaign. She had meetings with First Lady Hillary Clinton and provided advice on raising a child in the White House. Hillary Clinton considered Onassis a source of inspiration and advice during her time as First Lady.

SICKNESS, DEATH AND FUNERAL

Jacqueline Onassis faced health challenges in the later years of her life. In November 1993, she fell from a horse during a fox hunt, leading to the discovery of a swollen lymph node in her groin. Initially, it was thought to be caused by an infection, but in December, she developed new symptoms, including stomach pain and swollen lymph nodes in her neck. She was diagnosed with non-Hodgkin lymphoma, a type of blood cancer.

Despite starting chemotherapy in January 1994 and remaining optimistic about her prognosis, the cancer had spread to her spinal cord, brain, and liver by May, and her condition was deemed terminal. On May 18, 1994, she passed away in her sleep at her Manhattan apartment, surrounded by her children.

Her funeral Mass was held at the Church of St. Ignatius Loyola in New York City, where she had been baptized and confirmed. She was buried at Arlington National Cemetery in Virginia, alongside her first husband, President Kennedy, and their two deceased children.

Jacqueline Onassis' death was mourned by many, and President Bill Clinton delivered a eulogy at her graveside service. Her estate was valued at $43.7 million.

LEGACY
POPULARITY

Jacqueline Kennedy's marriage to Aristotle Onassis was met with significant disapproval from the American public, who viewed it as a betrayal of her late husband, President Kennedy. Many felt that her lavish lifestyle as Onassis's "trophy wife" contradicted the image of the selfless and devoted First Lady that the public had admired. The press portrayed her as a spendthrift and reckless woman.

However, over time, Jacqueline Onassis took control of her public image and worked to rehabilitate it. By returning to New York City after Onassis's death, focusing on her family and career as an editor, and participating in charitable causes, she managed to reshape her image. She also reestablished her ties with the Kennedy family and actively supported the John F. Kennedy Library and Museum.

Despite the initial public backlash, Jacqueline Onassis remains one of the most popular First Ladies in history. She consistently appeared on Gallup's annual list of the top 10 most admired people of the second half of the 20th century, a recognition surpassed by only a few individuals such as Billy Graham and Queen Elizabeth II. Her popularity among the American public endured, and her influence even extended to other prominent figures like Tina Turner and Jackie Joyner-Kersee, who cited her as an inspiration.

FASHION ICON

Jacqueline Kennedy became a global fashion icon during her time as First Lady. She commissioned Oleg Cassini, a French-born American fashion designer and Kennedy family friend, to create her wardrobe for official appearances. Cassini dressed her in numerous ensembles, including her Inauguration Day coat and gala gown, as well as outfits for her international visits.

Kennedy had a preference for French couture, especially designs from Chanel, Balenciaga, and Givenchy. However, she understood the importance of promoting American designers while serving as First Lady. To strike a balance, she sought recommendations from fashion editor Diana Vreeland for American designers who could reproduce the Parisian style she loved. Norman

Norell, Ben Zuckerman, and Stella Sloat were among those recommended to her.

Kennedy's signature style as First Lady included clean-cut suits with skirts down to the middle of the knee, three-quarter sleeves on notch-collar jackets, sleeveless A-line dresses, above-the-elbow gloves, low-heel pumps, and pillbox hats. This classic and sophisticated "Jackie" look quickly became a fashion trend worldwide. Her bouffant hairstyle, created by Mr. Kenneth, also gained immense popularity and was emulated by many. Additionally, her choice of eyewear, especially the oversized, oval-lensed sunglasses designed by François Pinton, became known as "Jackie O glasses" and is still referenced today.

Her fashion choices were widely copied by commercial manufacturers and inspired a generation of young women. Jacqueline Kennedy's influence on fashion was profound, and her enduring style legacy continues to be celebrated.

Jacqueline Kennedy Onassis was known for her style transformation after the White House, which included wide-leg pantsuits, silk Hermès headscarves, and large, round, dark sunglasses. She even began wearing jeans in public, setting a new fashion trend with beltless, white jeans and a black turtleneck that was never tucked in.

Kennedy had a large collection of jewelry, including a triple-strand pearl necklace designed by American jeweler Kenneth Jay Lane and a two-fruit cluster brooch of rubies with diamond stems and leaves, designed by French jeweler Jean Schlumberger for Tiffany & Co. She was also fond of Schlumberger's gold and enamel bracelets and white enamel and gold "banana" earrings.

As a Catholic, Kennedy was known for wearing a mantilla at Mass and in the presence of the Pope, and is credited with popularizing the veil among traditionalist Catholics. Mary Tyler Moore's character Laura Petrie on The Dick Van Dyke Show was often dressed like Kennedy, symbolizing the "feel-good nature" of the Kennedy White House.

Kennedy was inducted into the International Best Dressed List Hall of Fame in 1965, and many of her signature clothes are preserved at the John F. Kennedy Library and Museum. In 2012, Time magazine included her on its All-TIME 100 Fashion Icons list, and in 2016, Forbes included her on the list 10 Fashion Icons and the Trends They Made Famous.

HISTORICAL ASSESSMENTS

Jacqueline Kennedy Onassis has been highly regarded and celebrated for her role as First Lady and her contributions to American history and art. In 1962, she was named Time magazine's Woman of the Year for her efforts in uplifting American history and art.

Her popularity and appeal are attributed to various factors. Her sense of mystery and withdrawal from the public eye made her immensely appealing to the public. Despite her privilege, she became an aspirational figure that many Americans could strive to emulate. Her work in restoring the White House was widely praised and admired by various commentators and historians.

Over the years, surveys conducted by the Siena College Research Institute have consistently ranked

Jacqueline Kennedy Onassis among the most highly regarded first ladies. Her intelligence, courage, accomplishments, integrity, and leadership have contributed to her lasting legacy and positive perception by historians and the public alike.

Her influence as a fashion icon and her significant contributions to historic preservation, cultural diplomacy, and charitable causes have also contributed to her enduring popularity and admiration. Jacqueline Kennedy Onassis remains a prominent and respected figure in American history and continues to inspire and influence people around the world.

The Siena College Research Institute surveys have consistently shown Jacqueline Kennedy Onassis to be highly regarded and ranked among the top First Ladies in various categories. Over the years, her rankings improved significantly, with historians recognizing her achievements, leadership, courage, and value to the country.

In the 2008 survey, Onassis received high rankings in almost all criteria, particularly excelling in areas such as background, intelligence, value to the country, and public image. Her status as a "power couple" with her first husband, President John F. Kennedy, was also recognized.

While the 1982 survey ranked her lower in integrity, subsequent surveys showed a notable improvement in historians' views of her integrity. This shift in perception was likely influenced by her actions after her second widowhood, during which she demonstrated her independence through her successful career in publishing.

Overall, Jacqueline Kennedy Onassis's legacy as a First Lady and her contributions to American history and culture continue to be highly regarded, and she remains one of the most respected and admired figures in American history.

HONORS

Jacqueline Kennedy Onassis's legacy is honored through various institutions, landmarks, and awards. Some of these include:

- Jacqueline Kennedy Onassis High School for International Careers in New York City.

- Public School 66 in Queens, New York, renamed in her honor.

- The Jacqueline Kennedy Onassis Reservoir in Central Park, New York City.

- The Jacqueline Kennedy Onassis Foyer at Grand Central Terminal in New York City.

- The Jacqueline Kennedy Onassis Medal, presented by the Municipal Art Society of New York to individuals who contribute to the city's architecture and preservation.

- Jacqueline Bouvier Kennedy Onassis Hall at George Washington University, her alma mater.

- The Jacqueline Kennedy Garden, formerly the East Garden, at the White House.

- Inclusion of her and her first husband's names on the Kaguya and Lunar Reconnaissance Orbiter missions to the Moon.

- A school and award named after her at the American Ballet Theatre.

- Her involvement in the creation of the book "The Power of Myth" and its dedication to her.

- A white gazebo dedicated to her in Middleburg, Virginia, where she spent time with President Kennedy.

These honors and tributes reflect her significant impact on American history, preservation efforts, and her enduring influence as a fashion icon and cultural figure.

PORTRAYALS

Jacqueline Kennedy Onassis has been portrayed by several actresses in various films and television productions, each capturing different aspects of her life and legacy. Some notable portrayals include:

- Jaclyn Smith in the 1981 television film "Jacqueline Bouvier Kennedy," depicting her life until the end of JFK's presidency. Smith's performance received mixed reviews.

- Blair Brown in the 1983 miniseries "Kennedy," set during the Kennedy presidency. Brown's performance was praised, and she received award nominations.

- Roma Downey, Marianna Bishop, and Sarah Michelle Gellar in the 1991 miniseries "A Woman Named Jackie," covering her entire life until the death of Aristotle Onassis. Downey's performance received praise, and the miniseries won an Emmy Award.

- Jill Hennessy in the 2001 television film "Jackie, Ethel, Joan: The Women of Camelot." Hennessy's portrayal was well-received, bringing elegance to the role.

- Natalie Portman in the 2016 film "Jackie," set during JFK's presidency and the aftermath of his assassination. Portman's performance was widely acclaimed, earning her an Academy Award nomination for Best Actress.

- Jodi Balfour in the 2017 episode of Netflix's series "The Crown," titled "Dear Mrs. Kennedy," depicting the Kennedy couple's visit to Buckingham Palace and the reaction to JFK's assassination.

- Marianna Bishop, Sarah Michelle Gellar, and Roma Downey portrayed Jacqueline Kennedy Onassis in the 1991 miniseries "A Woman Named Jackie," covering her entire life until the death of Aristotle Onassis. Roma Downey's performance received praise, and the miniseries won an Emmy Award.

- Rhoda Griffis portrayed Jacqueline Kennedy in the 1992 film "Love Field," which is set shortly before and after JFK's assassination.

Each portrayal offers a unique perspective on Jacqueline Kennedy Onassis's life and contributions, and the performances have been subject to both praise and criticism from critics and audiences alike.

Printed in Great Britain
by Amazon

33609877R00046